WedgeWorks

by

Cheryl Phillips

with

Linda Pysto

This book is dedicated to my husband and best friend, Gary Phillips.

Thank you for your support and encouragement:
Brooke Phillips
Tom, Nicholas and Ben Pysto
Jeff, Roby and Arlene Vogel and the staff of Hi Fashion
    Fabrics, Grand Junction, Colorado.
Susan Rhyne
Meg Edwards, Irene Finnin, Jeanne Hunter, Sandy Low and Rhonda Schmeltzer
    for reading the manuscript.

Thank you for testing my patterns:
Becky Phillips
Lisa Castro
Charlene Edwards
Marcia Graham
Rita Larsen
Karla Schulz
The Colorado West Quilting Guild
Bev's Stitchery, Buena Vista, Colorado

A special thank you to: E&P Sewing, Gunnison, Colorado, publisher of *Quilts Without Corners.*

Acknowledgements:
Printed by Pyramid Printing, Grand Junction, Colorado
Photography by Dillard Jenkins of Colorado Photo Design, Grand Junction, Colorado

Table of Contents

                                                        Page

General Instructions 5

Citrus Placemats 7

Watermelon Placemats 7

Mini Tree Skirt 8

Striped Sampler 10

Poinsettia 18

China Blue Sampler 18

Pinwheel 19

Dresden Plate 29

Amish Spiral 32

Blue Corn Moon 34

Seed Packet 35

Birdhouse Banner 39

Sunny Side Up 39

Persian Star 40

Santa Banner 44

The Author

Cheryl Phillips lives in Fruita, Colorado with her husband Gary, and youngest daughter, Brooke. Cheryl is a national teacher, an innovative designer and a prolific quilter. Designs based on circles are a favorite of Cheryl's. *WedgeWorks* is her second book of circular designs following *Quilts Without Corners*. Cheryl's insatiable curiosity is expressed in her writing, teaching and quilting. She challenges herself and her students to nurture and develop their own creativity.

The Contributor

Linda Pysto lives in Las Vegas, Nevada with her husband Tom, and their sons Nicholas and Ben. She is an inspiring quilting teacher who thrives on seeing beginning students get hooked on the many possibilities found in quilting. Linda helped with the sewing, designing, and editing of *WedgeWorks*. Linda's supportive character serves to enhance the work of others.

The Friendship

Cheryl and Linda spent numerous weeks visiting each other, working side by side on this project. In the midst they discovered the joy of sharing the task: spinning ideas off one another, eating popcorn, laughing, eating popcorn, talking, eating popcorn, creating, eating popcorn. As the stack of projects grew, so too did their friendship...

a tribute to the power of quilting and the love of popcorn.

Dear Quilting Friend,

I had so much fun making the quilts in WedgeWorks. I hope you will too. The 15 degree wedge tool offers new challenges and design possibilities. Twenty four wedges fill a circle and 24 is a magical number! It's divisible by 2, 3, 4, 6, 8, and 12.

In addition to the projects within the covers of this book, you can further your own creative journey with circular 15 degree graph paper and a longer variation of the wedge tool. Information for ordering the WedgeWorks products is found on the inside of the back cover.

The projects I have included in WedgeWorks vary in complexity, with the simpler ones first and the more challenging ones later. While none are considered beginning projects, I encourage you to tackle them once you've tried your hand at some basic quilting. Basic classes are offered through local quilt guilds and shops. A number of beginning level books are also available to help you with basic rotary cutting and piecing. If you are an old hand at quilting and ready for a new direction, then this book is for you.

I have added folded inserts to many of my projects. Folding techniques add a third dimension to the designs while often making a complex design simpler to accomplish.

Please enjoy the projects as they are or feel free to give them your own twist with new colors, new fabrics, new sizes and new shapes. Ask yourself the infamous question that spurs us all toward new horizons:
What if I.....???

Happy wedge working,
Cheryl

General Instructions

Wedge Tool

The acrylic wedge tool provided in WedgeWorks is based on a 15 degree angle. The Wedge Tool includes a 1/4" seam allowance. You will need 24 fabric wedges to complete your circle.

Several of the patterns in this book require transferring placement lines onto the tool itself. I suggest you trace the lines with a fine tipped permanent marker. Place the wedge tool over the wedge diagram. Next, place a straight edge ruler on top and trace the line precisely. When you have completed your project these markings can be removed with acetone based finger nail polish remover.

I also recommend placing several loops of wide transparent packaging tape, sticky side out, onto the back of the wedge tool. This is an important step to assure accurate cutting because it keeps the tool from slipping even a tiny amount.

Templates

Several template patterns are included for the designs using folded inserts. You can make the templates yourself using template plastic (available at quilting stores) or purchase acrylic templates from the author (see inside back cover). Trace all lines and markings onto the templates.

Cutting Strips

All yardage calculations are based on 42" to 44" wide fabric. Strips are cut across the width of the fabric from selvage to selvage, unless specified otherwise. Be sure to straighten your fabric before cutting strips.

Sewing

Use **exact** 1/4" seams throughout. Do not assume your presser foot is an exact 1/4" wide. Test and measure to be certain. **Accuracy is crucial for your success.**

Sewing Strip Sets

Sew strip sets together being careful not to stretch as you sew. Remember that fabric widths vary so your sets will not end up being even on the end.

Sewing Wedges

The sides of the fabric wedges are bias and thus prone to stretch. Match and pin both ends to avoid stretching wedges. Be careful not to let the narrow end slip under the presser foot as you sew. The 1/4" seam allowance must be consistent along the entire length of the wedge.

Sewing Parallel 1/4" Bands

Straight parallel 1/4" bands are made much easier when you follow these tips:

Sew the 3/4" wide strip to the adjoining strip using exact 1/4" seam.

Pin the sewn strip on top of the next strip, right sides together.

Place the fabric strips to the **right** of the presser foot.

Sew along the length, aligning the edge of the 1/4" presser foot with **the previous stitching as a guide.**

Although this will seem a bit awkward at first, it does work. Do not be concerned if the second seam allowance is not exactly 1/4" wide, it is more important to have the width of the **sewn** strip be exactly 1/4" wide.

Pressing Designs Without Inserts

For designs without inserts, press after the half circle has been assembled. Press first from the back, pressing the seam allowances to one side. Next, press from the front. Press carefully to avoid tucks along the seam lines, but not so aggressively that your pieces are distorted or stretched.

Pressing Designs With Inserts

For designs with inserts, press each time an insert is added between wedges. Press first from the back, laying the inserts to one side and opening the seam allowances. This takes a bit more time, but it is helpful in getting the inserts centered and lying flat. Next, press from the front. Open up the insert and center the insert fold line over the wedge seam you've just sewn. To make the inserted points sharp, roll the point between your fingers to shape and center it.

Checking Halves

Before sewing half circles together, check to see that your half is a true 180 degrees.

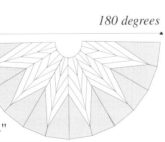

180 degrees

If not, first examine your seam allowances to see that they are exactly 1/4" wide. Sometimes the wedge seam slips at the narrow end. If so, correct the seams and repress.

Often the problem is due to over-pressing. You **can** undo stretching with blocking. Position the circle half on the ironing board so the top edge is straight. Using the steam setting on your iron, reshape the half circle with gentle pats.

Center Appliques

Stabilize the center opening from the back of the circular block by ironing a square of freezer paper over the opening.

Trace the applique pattern suggested in the design onto the dull side of a piece of freezer paper. Cut out the paper pattern. Compare the applique to the opening in the pieced circle. It should extend beyond the edge of the opening by 1/4" all around. Adjust the size if needed.

Press the shiny side of the freezer paper pattern onto the **wrong** side of the applique fabric. Cut the applique fabric 1/4" from the edge of the paper. Apply glue stick along the edge of the paper applique. Wrap the fabric over the paper edge. Center and pin the applique over the opening. Hand or machine stitch the circle applique in place. Remove all freezer paper.

Corners

Mark the notches onto the corner pieces. Match the markings with the wedge seams. Sew the corner to the circle, always placing the circle against the bed of the machine with the corner unit on top.

Quilt Assembly

Check to see if the blocks are truly square. Adjust as necessary.

Sew lattice strips to the blocks where indicated.

Sew triangles to the blocks which are set on point.

Sew the blocks together in rows as shown in the individual diagrams.

Sew the rows together to make the quilt top.

Sew the borders to the pieced top.

Finishing

When the project is pieced you are ready to quilt and bind it. Layer the backing, batting and project top. Pin the layers together. Quilt as desired.

I hope you will find the WedgeWorks' projects an excellent opportunity to display your quilting skills. There are many reference books on hand and machine quilting.

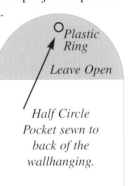

Plastic Ring

Leave Open

Half Circle Pocket sewn to back of the wallhanging.

Curved edges need to be bound with **bias** binding. You may use straight-cut binding for straight edges.

Hanging curved wallhangings can be challenging. A pocket to hold a curved cardboard cut-out can be sewn to the backing to support the curved edge. Sew on a plastic ring for hanging.

Watermelon Placemat

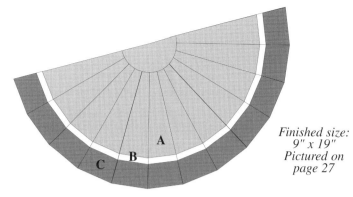

*Finished size:
9" x 19"
Pictured on
page 27*

For two placemats:

Fabric	Yardage	Strips to Cut
A	1/3 yd	ONE . . . . . . .8" wide strip
B	1/8 yd	TWO . . . .3/4" wide strips
C	1/4 yd	TWO . . . . . .2" wide strips
Backing	3/8 yd	
Batting	3/8 yd	

For more placemats:

Fabric	Yardage		
	Four	Six	Eight
A	1/2 yd	3/4 yd	1 yd
B	1/8 yd	1/4 yd	1/4 yd
C	3/8 yd	3/8 yd	1/2 yd
Strip Sets	2	3	4
Backing	5/8 yd	1 yd	1 1/4 yd
Batting	5/8 yd	1 yd	1 1/4 yd

Sewing Strip Sets

• Sew the strips together to form a strip set.
Need help getting the 1/4" bands straight and even? See page 6.

• From the back, press the strip set with the seam allowances toward the C Fabric.

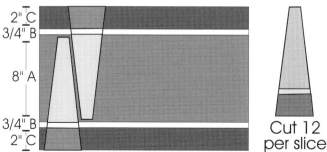

2" C
3/4" B

8" A

3/4" B
2" C

Cut 12
per slice

You must keep the wedge cuts very close together so you'll have enough fabric for two mats.

Cutting Wedges

• Place the Wedge Tool on the strip set.
• Cut *twelve* fabric wedges for each placemat.

Sewing the Half Circle

• Place wedge pairs together, matching the seam lines.
• Pin at the seam lines.
• Sew a wedge pair together.
• Continue sewing wedges for a half circle of *twelve* wedges.

Pressing the Half Circle

• From the back, press seam allowances to one side.
• Press again from the front.

Center Applique

• Prepare the half circle applique on page 47.
• Applique the half circle over the center opening.

Finishing

• Place the backing fabric onto a piece of batting.
• Pin the half circle slice onto the backing fabric, right sides together.
• Sew around the edge of the watermelon slice, leaving an opening for turning.
• Cut away the backing fabric and batting to match the half circle.
• Turn to the right side.
• Hand stitch the opening closed.
• Quilt as desired.

Another flavor?
See the Citrus Placemats on page 27.

Mini Christmas Tree Skirt

Fabric	Yardage	Strips to Cut
A	1/2 yd	SIX . . . . . 2 1/2" wide strips
B	5/8 yd	THREE . . . . .3" wide strips
C*	1/4 yd	SIX . . . . . . .3/4" wide strips
Ruffle	3/8 yd	THREE . . . . .3" wide strips
Backing	5/8 yd	

If Fabric C choice is Lamé, back with woven fusible interfacing.

Interfacing* 1/4 yd

Finished Size: 20"circle

Pictured on Page 23

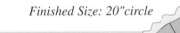

Cutting Strips

Note: Strips are cut across the fabric width (44-45").

• Cut fabric strips as listed.

Sewing Strip Sets

• Sew the strips together to make three strip sets.

Need help getting the 1/4" bands straight and even? See page 6.

• Press the strip sets from both the back and front so the seams lie flat without tucks. Lamé 1/4" bands are difficult to force in a particular direction, so just let them have their own way.

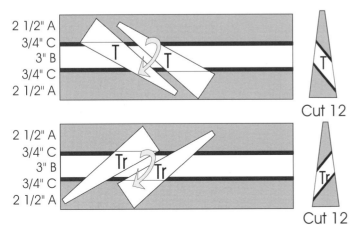

2 1/2" A
3/4" C
3" B
3/4" C
2 1/2" A

T   T

Cut 12

2 1/2" A
3/4" C
3" B
3/4" C
2 1/2" A

Tr   Tr

Cut 12

Cutting Wedges

• Mark line T, page 9, onto the Wedge Tool.

• Place the Wedge Tool onto the strip set, matching line T with the AC seam.

• Cut *twelve* T wedges from one strip set.

• Cut *twelve* Tr wedges from the other strip set.

T   mirror image   Tr

Note: The Tr wedges are the mirror image of the T wedges.

Sewing Wedge Pairs

• Pin two wedges together, matching the seams.

• Sew twelve wedge pairs together.

Sewing Foursies

• Pin two wedge pairs together, matching seams.

• Sew wedge pairs together to make a unit of four wedges, a "foursie".

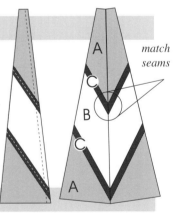

match seams

Sewing Half Circles

• Pin two foursies together, matching seams.

• Sew the foursies together.

• Add a third foursie to make a half circle.

• Press the seam allowances to one side.

• Repeat for the other half circle.

180 degrees

If adjustment is necessary, see page 6 for suggestions.

Pressing Half Circles

• Press the half circle carefully.
• Check to see that the half circle is straight.
• Repeat for the other half circle.

Ruffle

• Sew *three* 3" wide strips together making one long strip.

Sew here

Fold

• Sew along the ends with right sides together.
• Fold the strip in half lengthwise, wrong sides together, and press.
• Sew the ends as shown.
• Stitch 1/4" from the edge using a gathering stitch.
• Pin the ruffle to the circle, raw edges together.
• Adjust the gathers to distribute fullness.
• Sew the ruffle to the circle.

Backing

• Pin the tree skirt onto a 20" square of backing fabric with the right sides together, sandwiching the ruffle.
• Sew around the circle directly on top of the gathering stitches.
• Sew along the sides and center opening, leaving an opening for turning.
• Cut away the excess backing fabric.
• Turn the tree skirt to the right side.
• Hand stitch the opening closed.

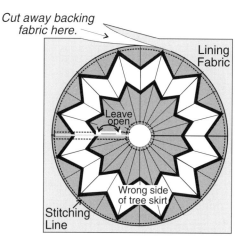

Cut away backing fabric here.

Lining Fabric

Leave open

Wrong side of tree skirt

Stitching Line

Creative Option

The Mini Tree Skirt makes a decorative Table Topper when you applique a 2"circle over the center opening. Make the Table Topper in a variety of colors for use any time of the year.

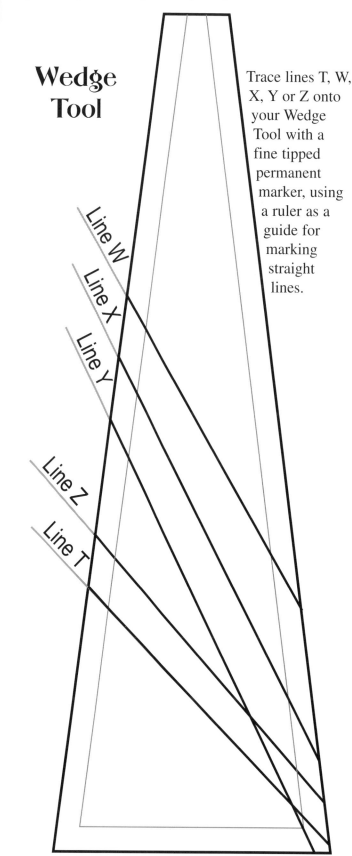

Wedge Tool

Trace lines T, W, X, Y or Z onto your Wedge Tool with a fine tipped permanent marker, using a ruler as a guide for marking straight lines.

Line W
Line X
Line Y
Line Z
Line T

Fabric Selection

Consider any striped fabric--even, uneven, linear prints, or border designs. When you purchase yardage, keep in mind both the number and frequency of stripe or design repeats. Buy a few extra yards if you want to focus on certain portions of the stripe. I used ten yards of the wavy striped fabric in my Striped Sampler quilt pictured on page 26.

The Sampler designs are not limited to just stripes. A variety of print fabrics can be equally as lovely as shown in the Poinsettia pictured on page 23.

Strong contrasts in value will accentuate the piecing lines as shown in the China Blue Sampler pictured on page 28.

Yardage

A (Accent fabric)	. . . .	.1/4 yd
B (Background)	. . . .	.4 3/4 yd
C (Corner pieces)	. . . .	.2 3/4 yd
S* (Stripe)	. . . .	6 to 10 yd

*See 'Fabric Selection' above.

S (If fabric choice is not a stripe)	. . .	4 1/2 yd
L (Lattice)	. . . .	.5/8 yd
Border 1	. . . .	.5/8 yd
Border 2	. . . .	.1 1/8 yd
Binding	. . . .	.3/4 yd

Cutting Strips

It is important to first establish grain line with respect to the direction of the stripe. Lengthwise stripes are parallel to the selvage. Crosswise stripes are perpendicular to the selvage.

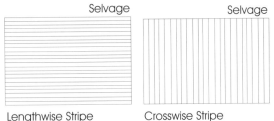

Cut the fabric strips listed in the cutting chart for each block. Be aware of the stripe placement in each block diagram. The stripes are vertical for blocks #2, #3 and #9 and horizontal for the remaining blocks.

STRIPED SAMPLER

The Striped Sampler is made of twelve 20" blocks.
The finished quilt measures 71" x 91".

22" wide strips

If making only one block, cut the 22" strips as indicated in the block directions and butt the 22" strips together.

If making several blocks, you may want to first cut 44" strips along the lengthwise grain to eliminate waste.

Cutting Lattice and Borders

Fabric S	NINE	. . . . .1 1/2" strips
	FOUR	. . . . . .4 1/2" squares
Fabric B	SIX	. . . . .1 1/2" squares
	EIGHT	. . . . . . .4 1/2" strips

Sewing Strip Sets

Sew strip sets in the order shown in each block diagram. From the back, press the strip set seam allowances to one side. Press again from the front to eliminate any tucks along the seams.

Preparing the Wedge Tool

Trace lines W, X, Y and Z (see page 9) onto the Wedge Tool using a fine permanent marker. Place loops of wide transparent tape, sticky side out, onto the back of the Wedge Tool.

Cutting Wedges

Place the Wedge Tool onto the strip set. Align line W, X, Y or Z with the corresponding seam line following the individual block diagram. Precision is crucial. Cut one wedge, then rotate the Wedge Tool to cut the wedge above or below the first one. You *must* cut the wedge above or below the first *before* moving across the strip set. Leave *very little* fabric between wedges.

Cutting Mirror Image Wedges

Some blocks require cutting mirror image wedges. This will be indicated by the lower case letter '**r**'. To cut a mirror image wedge, place tape on the *opposite* side and then turn the Wedge Tool over. Check carefully before cutting to be certain the new wedge is *truly* the mirror image of the others.

Sewing Circles

• Lay out the wedges as shown in each block diagram.

Pairs

• Pin a wedge pair with right sides together, matching seams.

• Sew the wedges together.

• Sew *twelve* wedge pairs per block.

• Return the wedge pairs to the circle layout.

Foursies

• Sew the wedge pairs together to make six units of four wedges, "foursies".

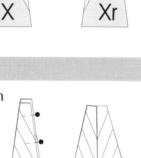

a foursie

Half Circle

• Sew *three* foursies together to make a half circle.

• Press the half circle from the back, with seam allowances going in one direction.

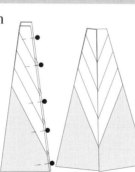

Half Circle

180 degrees

• Check to see that the half circle is straight.

• Repeat for the other half circle.

If adjustment is necessary, see page 6 for suggestions.

Circle

• Sew the halves together to make a circle.

• Press the seam allowances to one side.

• Repeat for a total of *twelve* blocks.

Appliqueing Centers

• Prepare the 2" circle applique found on page 47.

• Applique the circle over the center opening.

• For more information see page 6.

Adding Corners

• Fold the 12" Fabric C square diagonally.

• Place the Corner-19 Template along the fold of Fabric C.

• Cut *four* corner pieces.

• Sew the *four* corner pieces together.

• Pin the corner unit to the circle, matching seams and notches.

• Sew the corner unit to the circle with the circle against the bed of the sewing machine.

• Press the seam allowances toward the outside of the block.

Assembling the Blocks

• Sew the 1 1/2" Fabric S lattice strips and the 1 1/2" Fabric B squares to the blocks as shown in the quilt diagram.

• Sew the blocks together in rows.

• Sew the rows together to make the quilt top.

• Join the 4 1/2" strips of Fabric B together in pairs.

• Measure the sides of the pieced quilt.

• Cut the strips to these lengths.

• Sew on the 4 1/2" Fabric S squares to the border strips.

BLOCK 1

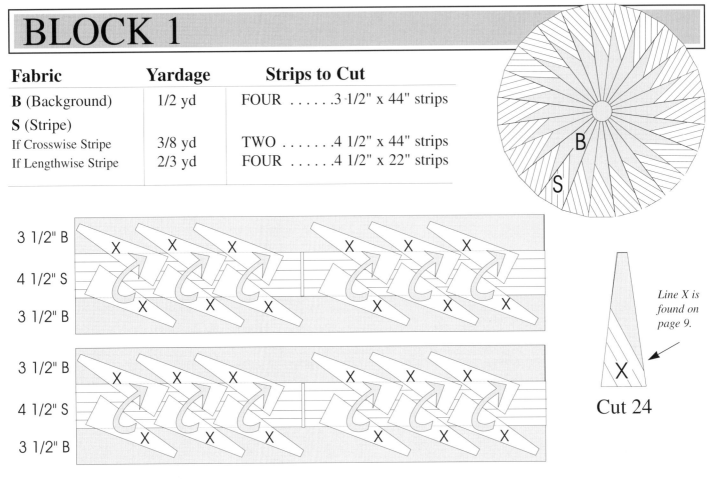

Fabric	Yardage	Strips to Cut
B (Background)	1/2 yd	FOUR . . . . . .3 1/2" x 44" strips
S (Stripe)		
If Crosswise Stripe	3/8 yd	TWO . . . . . . .4 1/2" x 44" strips
If Lengthwise Stripe	2/3 yd	FOUR . . . . . .4 1/2" x 22" strips

3 1/2" B
4 1/2" S
3 1/2" B

3 1/2" B
4 1/2" S
3 1/2" B

Line X is found on page 9.

Cut 24

BLOCK 2

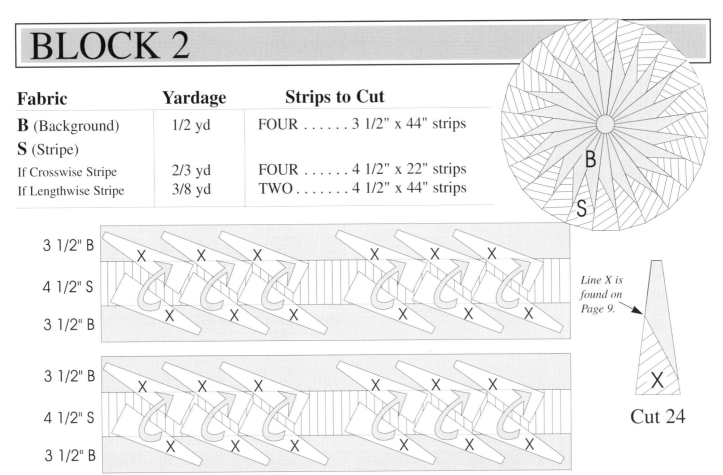

Fabric	Yardage	Strips to Cut
B (Background)	1/2 yd	FOUR . . . . . . 3 1/2" x 44" strips
S (Stripe)		
If Crosswise Stripe	2/3 yd	FOUR . . . . . . 4 1/2" x 22" strips
If Lengthwise Stripe	3/8 yd	TWO . . . . 4 1/2" x 44" strips

3 1/2" B
4 1/2" S
3 1/2" B

3 1/2" B
4 1/2" S
3 1/2" B

Line X is found on Page 9.

Cut 24

BLOCK 3

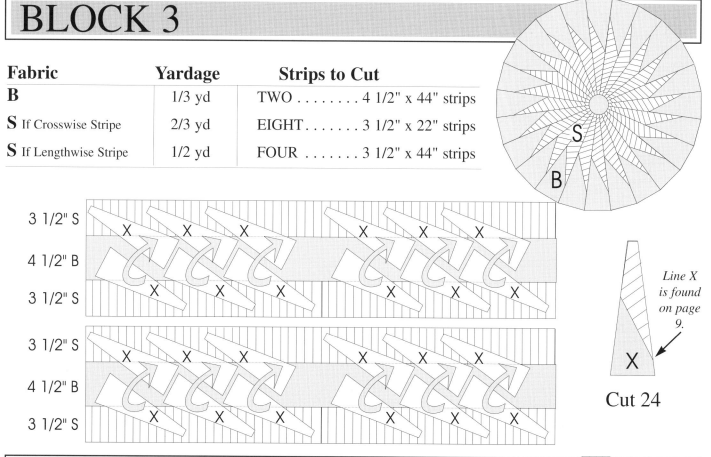

Fabric	Yardage	Strips to Cut
B	1/3 yd	TWO . . . . 4 1/2" x 44" strips
S If Crosswise Stripe	2/3 yd	EIGHT . . . . 3 1/2" x 22" strips
S If Lengthwise Stripe	1/2 yd	FOUR . . . . 3 1/2" x 44" strips

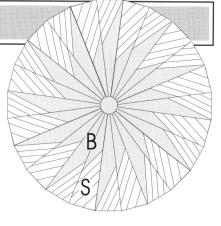

Line X is found on page 9.

Cut 24

BLOCK 4

Fabric	Yardage	Strips to Cut
B	1/2 yd	FOUR . . . . .3 1/2" x 44" strips
S If Crosswise Stripe	3/8 yd	ONE . . . . .4 1/2" x 44" strip
		ONE . . . . .5 1/2" x 44" strip
S If Lengthwise Stripe	2/3 yd	TWO . . . . .4 1/2" x 22" strips
		TWO . . . . .5 1/2" x 22" strips

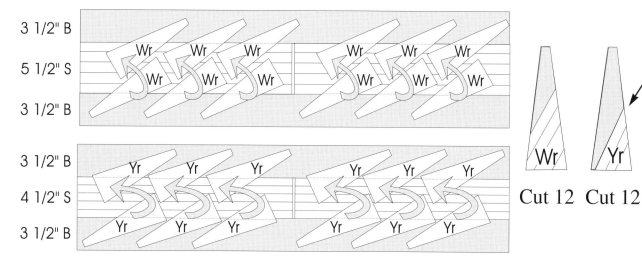

Lines W and Y are found on page 9.

Wr Yr

Cut 12 Cut 12

BLOCK 5

Fabric	Yardage	Strips to Cut
B	3/8 yd	ONE . . . . .4 1/2" x 44" strip
		ONE . . . . . . .5 1/2" x 44" strip
S If Crosswise Stripe	1/2 yd	FOUR . . . . . .3 1/2" x 44" strips
S If Lengthwise Stripe	2/3 yd	EIGHT . . . . . .3 1/2" x 22" strips

3 1/2" S
5 1/2" B
3 1/2" S

Wr Wr Wr   Wr Wr Wr
Wr Wr Wr   Wr Wr Wr

3 1/2" S
4 1/2" B
3 1/2" S

Yr Yr Yr   Yr Yr Yr
Yr Yr Yr   Yr Yr Yr

Wr Cut 12

Yr Cut 12

Lines W and Y are found on page 9.

BLOCK 6

Fabric	Yardage	Strips to Cut
B	1/3 yd	TWO . . . . .4 1/2" x 44" strips
S If Crosswise Stripe	1/2 yd	FOUR . . . . .3 1/2" x 44" strips
S If Lengthwise Stripe	2/3 yd	EIGHT . . . . 3 1/2" x 22" strips

3 1/2" S
4 1/2" B
3 1/2" S

X X X   X X X
X X X   X X X

mirror image

3 1/2" S
4 1/2" B
3 1/2" S

Xr Xr Xr   Xr Xr Xr
Xr Xr Xr   Xr Xr Xr

mirror

X Cut 12   **Xr** Cut 12

Line X is found on page 9.

BLOCK 7

Fabric	Yardage	Strips to Cut
B	3/8 yd	ONE . . . . .4 1/2" x 44" strip
		ONE . . . . .5 1/2" x 44" strip
S If Crosswise Stripe	1/2 yd	FOUR . . . . . . .3 1/2" x 44" strips
S If Lengthwise Stripe	2/3 yd	EIGHT . . . . . . .3 1/2" x 22" strips

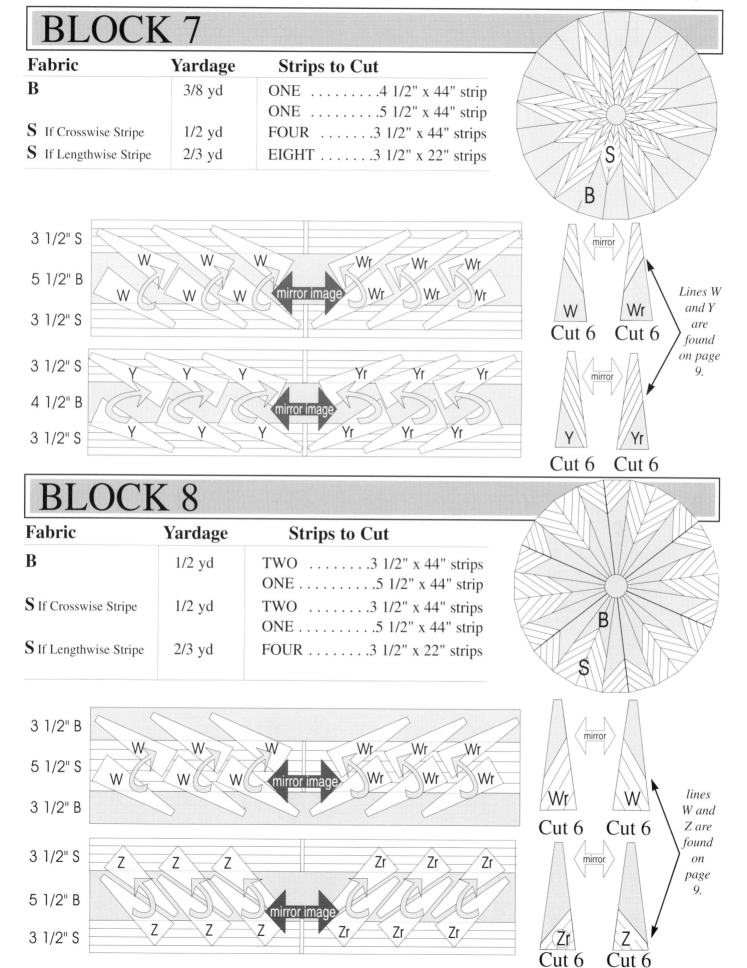

3 1/2" S

5 1/2" B

3 1/2" S

W W W   Wr Wr Wr
W W W   mirror image   Wr Wr Wr

3 1/2" S

4 1/2" B

3 1/2" S

Y Y Y   Yr Yr Yr
Y Y Y   mirror image   Yr Yr Yr

mirror

W   Wr
Cut 6   Cut 6

Lines W and Y are found on page 9.

mirror

Y   Yr
Cut 6   Cut 6

BLOCK 8

Fabric	Yardage	Strips to Cut
B	1/2 yd	TWO . . . . .3 1/2" x 44" strips
		ONE . . . . .5 1/2" x 44" strip
S If Crosswise Stripe	1/2 yd	TWO . . . . . . .3 1/2" x 44" strips
		ONE . . . . .5 1/2" x 44" strip
S If Lengthwise Stripe	2/3 yd	FOUR . . . . . . .3 1/2" x 22" strips

3 1/2" B

5 1/2" S

3 1/2" B

W W W   Wr Wr Wr
W W W   mirror image   Wr Wr Wr

3 1/2" S

5 1/2" B

3 1/2" S

Z Z Z   Zr Zr Zr
Z Z Z   mirror image   Zr Zr Zr

mirror

Wr   W
Cut 6   Cut 6

lines W and Z are found on page 9.

mirror

Zr   Z
Cut 6   Cut 6

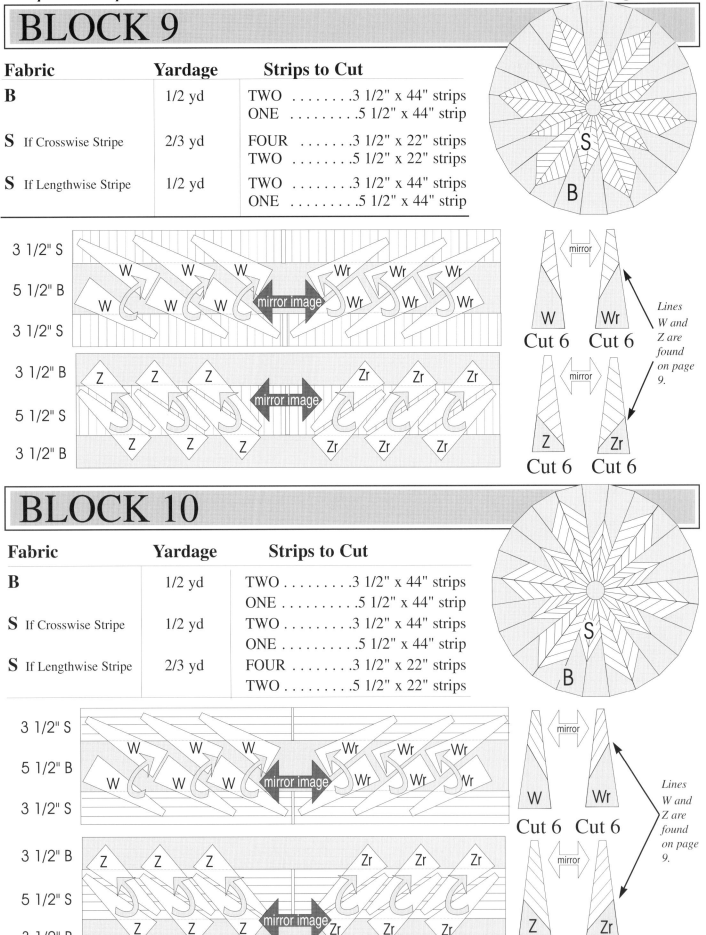

BLOCK 9

Fabric	Yardage	Strips to Cut
B	1/2 yd	TWO ....3 1/2" x 44" strips ONE ....5 1/2" x 44" strip
S If Crosswise Stripe	2/3 yd	FOUR ....3 1/2" x 22" strips TWO ......5 1/2" x 22" strips
S If Lengthwise Stripe	1/2 yd	TWO ....3 1/2" x 44" strips ONE ....5 1/2" x 44" strip

3 1/2" S
5 1/2" B
3 1/2" S

3 1/2" B
5 1/2" S
3 1/2" B

W W W mirror image Wr Wr Wr
Z Z Z mirror image Zr Zr Zr

Cut 6 Cut 6 W Wr
Cut 6 Cut 6 Z Zr

Lines W and Z are found on page 9.

BLOCK 10

Fabric	Yardage	Strips to Cut
B	1/2 yd	TWO ....3 1/2" x 44" strips ONE ....5 1/2" x 44" strip
S If Crosswise Stripe	1/2 yd	TWO ....3 1/2" x 44" strips ONE ....5 1/2" x 44" strip
S If Lengthwise Stripe	2/3 yd	FOUR ....3 1/2" x 22" strips TWO ....5 1/2" x 22" strips

3 1/2" S
5 1/2" B
3 1/2" S

3 1/2" B
5 1/2" S
3 1/2" B

W W W mirror image Wr Wr Wr
Z Z Z mirror image Zr Zr Zr

Cut 6 Cut 6 W Wr
Cut 6 Cut 6 Z Zr

Lines W and Z are found on page 9.

BLOCK 11

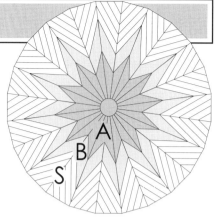

Fabric	Yardage	Strips to Cut
A	1/4 yd	TWO . . . . .3" x 44" strips
B	1/4 yd	FOUR . . . . . . .1 1/2" x 44" strips
S If Crosswise Stripe	1/2 yd	FOUR . . . . . . .3 1/2" x 44" strips
S If Lengthwise Stripe	2/3 yd	EIGHT . . . . . .3 1/2" x 22" strips

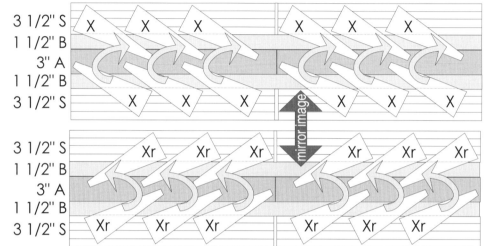

3 1/2" S
1 1/2" B
3" A
1 1/2" B
3 1/2" S

3 1/2" S
1 1/2" B
3" A
1 1/2" B
3 1/2" S

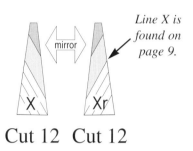

Line X is found on page 9.

Cut 12   Cut 12

BLOCK 12

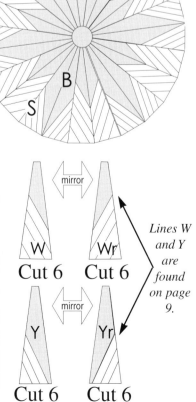

Fabric	Yardage	Strips to Cut
B	1/2 yd	FOUR . . . . . . .3 1/2" x 44" strips
S If Crosswise Stripe	3/8 yd	ONE . . . . .4 1/2" x 44" strip
		ONE . . . . .5 1/2" x 44" strip
S If Lengthwise Stripe	2/3 yd	TWO . . . . . . .4 1/2" x 22" strips
		TWO . . . . . . .5 1/2" x 22" strips

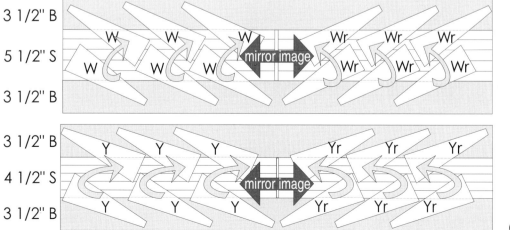

3 1/2" B
5 1/2" S
3 1/2" B

3 1/2" B
4 1/2" S
3 1/2" B

Cut 6   Cut 6

Lines W and Y are found on page 9.

Cut 6   Cut 6

The **Poinsettia**

*A Variation of the Striped Sampler Using Block #9. You can use this layout with **any** of the sampler blocks.*

Pictured on page 23

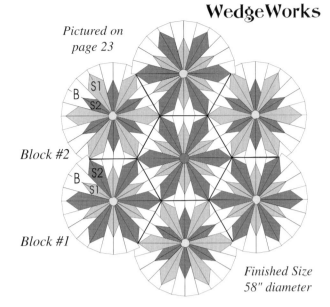

Yardage	
B . . . . .2 5/8 yd
S1 . . . . .1 5/8 yd
S2 . . . . .1 1/4 yd
Binding . . . . .3/4 yd
Batting . . . . .60" square
Backing . . . . .3 1/2 yd

Refer to the Striped Sampler Instructions pages 9 and 10, and Block #9, page 16.

Block #2

Block #1

Finished Size 58" diameter

#1 Blocks

- Cut fabric strips B and S1 for strip set W-Wr.
- Cut fabric strips B and S2 for strip set Z-Zr.
- Sew the strips sets.
- Cut *six* wedges of each: W, Wr, Z, and Zr.
- Sew the wedges together to make a #1 Block.
- Repeat for *four* #1 Blocks.

#2 Blocks

- Cut fabric strips B and S2 for strip set W-Wr.
- Cut fabric strips B and S1 for strip set Z-Zr.
- Sew the strips sets.
- Cut *six* wedges of each: W, Wr, Z, and Zr.
- Sew the wedges together to make a #2 Block.
- Repeat for *three* #2 Blocks.

- Mark *six* lines onto the back of the center block, drawing from point to point as shown.
- Mark *three* lines onto the back of the remaining blocks, drawing from point to point as shown.

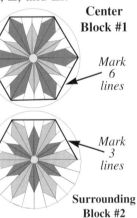

Center Block #1

Mark 6 lines

Mark 3 lines

Surrounding Block #2

- Pin one block on top of the center block, right sides together, placing the marked lines exactly on top of one another.
- Sew along the marked line stopping at the seam.
- Repeat sewing the remaining blocks to the center block, stopping at the seam.
- Place the adjacent blocks together, right sides facing, aligning the marked lines.
- Sew along the line.
- Repeat for the remaining blocks.

Place marked lines together

Sew first

Sew next

- Where blocks are joined, cut off the excess seam allowance 1/4" from the sewn line.

Back View

Cut away excess fabric.

- Refer to *Finishing* on page 6.

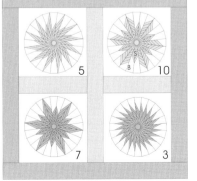

Pictured on page 28

China Blue Sampler

A Variation of the Striped Sampler Using Blocks #3, #5, #7, and #10

Finished Size 45" Square

*Use this layout with **any** of the sampler blocks.*

- Make blocks #3, #5, #7 and #10 following the *Striped Sampler* instructions.
- Sew the blocks together with 3" wide lattice strips.
- Border with 4" wide striped fabric strips.

the PinWheel

Fabric	Yardage	Pieces to Cut
Blades		
A1	3/8 yd	TWO . . . . .9 3/4" squares
A2	3/8 yd	TWO . . . . .9 3/4" squares
A3	3/8 yd	TWO . . . . .9 3/4" squares
A4	3/8 yd	TWO . . . . .9 3/4" squares
A5	3/8 yd	TWO . . . . .9 3/4" squares
A6	3/8 yd	TWO . . . . .9 3/4" squares
A2,A4,A6		ONE . . . . .1 3/4" strip of each
Background B	2 3/8 yd	TWO . . . . . .16" x 5 1/2" pieces*
		FOUR . . . . .6 1/2" strips**
		TWO . . . . . . .8 1/4" x 21" pieces
		FOUR . . . . . . .8 1/4" x 16" pieces
		SIX . . . . .9 1/2" squares
Interfacing	1 5/8 yd	TWELVE . . . . . . .9 1/4" squares
(Fusible)		
Batting	1 1/2 yd	*Cut these pieces first.*
Backing	1 1/2 yd	***Refer to the cutting*
Binding	1/8 yd each *A1-A6*	*diagram below.*

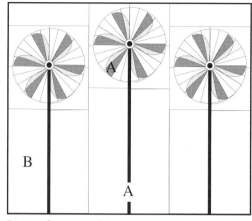

Pictured on page 21   Finished Size: 46" x 36"

Cutting Fabric Pieces

• Cut the A1 thru A6 fabric squares.

• Cut the background pieces following the suggested layout shown below.

• Cut the squares of fusible interfacing.

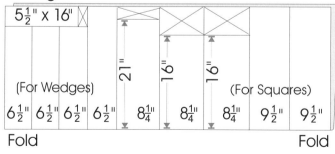

Selvages

5½" x 16"

(For Wedges)   21"   16"   16"   (For Squares)

6½"   6½"   6½"   6½"   8¼"   8¼"   8¼"   9½"   9½"

Fold   Fold

Cutting Corner Pieces

• Fold the 9 1/2" Fabric B squares diagonally.

• Place the Corner-14.5 Template, page 45, on the fold of Fabric B.

• Cut *twelve* corner pieces.

Fold   B   9 1/2"

Corner-14.5   9 1/2"

Cutting Wedges

• Apply loops of wide transparent tape, sticky side out, to the back of the Wedge Tool.

• Mark the *6 1/2" line* (found on page 44) on the Wedge Tool with a fine tipped permanent marker.

• Place the Wedge Tool on a 6 1/2" wide strip of Fabric B. Align the 6 1/2" line with the fabric edge.

• Cut *24* wedges.

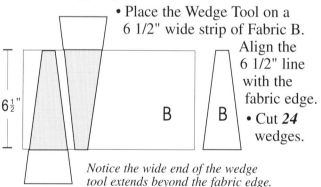

6½"

B   B

Notice the wide end of the wedge tool extends beyond the fabric edge.

Cutting Pinwheels

• Iron a square of interfacing onto the wrong side of the center of each pinwheel square, following manufacturer's directions.

• Select *two* colors for each pinwheel.

• Place the squares together in the chosen color combinations with right sides together.

• Cut the squares *twice* diagonally, cutting through both layers at once.

• Repeat for the remaining pairs.

cut on diagonals

interfacing

A

Sewing Wedge Pairs

- Place a wedge on top of another, right sides facing.
- Sew the wedges together to form a pair.
- Repeat, sewing *twelve* wedge pairs per block.
- Press the wedge pair seam allowances to one side.

Sewing Pinwheels

- Sew the pinwheel blades together along the long and one short side.
- Sew *six* blade sets for each block.
- Trim the sewn corner.
- Turn the blades right side out.
- Press the blades.

Note: You'll have two leftover blades per color combination.

Cut here

A

Pinwheel Blade

Sewing Foursies

- Place a pinwheel blade onto a wedge pair **1/4"** from the top edge as shown.
- Pin another wedge pair on top.

1/4" from top edge

A   A

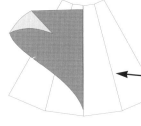

- Sew the wedge pairs together for a unit of four wedges, a "foursie".

Sewing Halves

- Place one foursie on top of another, right sides together.
- Sew the foursies together.
- Add a third foursie to make a half.

Adding Corners

- Sew two corner pieces together.
- Pin the corner unit onto the half circle, matching seams.
- Sew the corner to the half circle.
- Repeat for the remaining half circles.

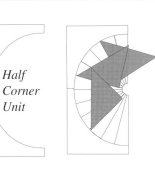

Half Corner Unit

Assembling the WallHanging

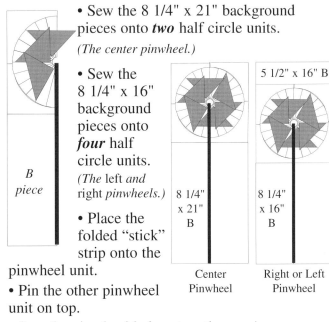

- Sew the 8 1/4" x 21" background pieces onto *two* half circle units. *(The center pinwheel.)*

- Sew the 8 1/4" x 16" background pieces onto *four* half circle units. *(The left and right pinwheels.)*

- Place the folded "stick" strip onto the pinwheel unit.

B piece

5 1/2" x 16" B

8 1/4" x 21" B

8 1/4" x 16" B

Center Pinwheel

Right or Left Pinwheel

- Pin the other pinwheel unit on top.
- Sew the pinwheel halves together.
- Sew the 5 1/2" x 16" background pieces onto the top of the left and right pinwheel blocks.

Finishing

- Sew the rectangular pinwheel sections together.
- Applique 2" circles over each center opening.
- Bring the tip of each pinwheel blade to the center of the pinwheel, arranging them to resemble an actual pinwheel.
- Sew a button through the pinwheel tips to hold the blades in place.

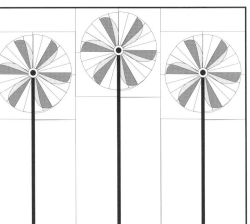

- See page 6 for additional finishing directions.

Creative Options

A Pinwheel Valance will brighten any child's room. Continue the fabric "sticks" onto a Roman Shade to complete the charming window treatment. For a coordinating Grow Chart, stitch a cloth measuring tape for the pinwheel stick.

Pinwheel
*designed and pieced by
Linda, quilted by Cheryl*

Sunny Side Up
a variation of the Seed Packet,
a combined effort of Cheryl and Linda

Birdhouse Banner
a variation of the Seed Packet
designed, pieced and quilted by Cheryl

21

Seed Packet
designed, pieced and quilted by Cheryl

Poinsettia
*a variation of the
Striped Sampler
pieced by Linda,
quilted by Cheryl*

Santa Banner
*designed, pieced and quilted
by Cheryl*

Mini Tree Skirt
*designed, pieced and
quilted by Cheryl*

Amish Spiral
designed, pieced and hand quilted by Linda

Blue Corn Moon
a variation of the Amish Spiral
designed, pieced and quilted by Linda

Persian Star
(left) designed, pieced and quilted by Cheryl

Striped Sampler
*(left) pieced by Linda
and Cheryl, designed
and quilted by Cheryl*

Watermelon
*designed, pieced and
quilted by Cheryl*

Citrus Placemats
*ideal for a summer luncheon,
a color variation of the* Watermelon
pieced and quilted by Linda

Dresden Plate
"Char's Star"
designed, pieced and
quilted by Cheryl

China Blue Sampler
a variation of the Striped Sampler
designed, pieced and quilted by Cheryl

Dresden Plate

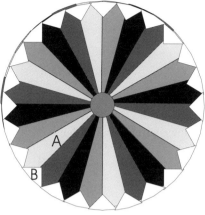

Pictured on page 28

Yardage

Fabric	Runner	Lap	Double	Queen/King
	3 blocks 22" x 66"	8 blocks 44" x 66"	18 blocks 78" x 100"	25 blocks 100" x 100"
24 Different Fabrics A1--A24	scraps	1/4 yd each	1/4 yd each	1/4 yd each
Borders	n/a	n/a	1/4 yd each	1/4 yd each
Background	1 2/3 yd	2 3/4 yd	5 yd	7 1/2 yd
Batting (90" wide)	3/4 yd	1 1/3 yd	3 yd	6 yd
Backing	2 yd	4 yd	6 yd	9 yd
Binding	3/8 yd	1/2 yd	3/4 yd	7/8 yd

Cutting

Fabric	Runner		Lap		Double		Queen/King	
A1-A24 24 different fabrics								
A (for wedges)	6 1/2" x 8" each		6 1/2" x 16" each		6 1/2" x 33" each		6 1/2" x 44" each	
A (for borders)	n/a		n/a		NINE 6 1/2" x 44"		TEN 6 1/2" x 44"	
B Background								
B (for block inserts)	SIX	2" x 44"	SIXTEEN	2" x 44"	THIRTY SIX	2" x 44"	FIFTY	2" x 44"
B (for border inserts)		n/a		n/a	SEVENTEEN	2" x 44"	EIGHTEEN	2" x 44"
B (squares)	TWO	11 1/2" sq	TWO	11 1/2" sq	TWO	11 1/2" sq	TWO	11 1/2" sq
	ONE	22 1/2" sq	TWO	22 1/2" sq	THREE	22 1/2" sq	THREE	22 1/2" sq
B (for corners)	SIX	9 1/2" sq	SIXTEEN	9 1/2" sq	THIRTY SIX	9 1/2" sq	FIFTY	9 1/2" sq

Cutting Background Pieces

Refer to the Cutting Chart for the number of squares needed.

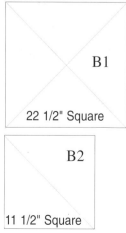

B1

22 1/2" Square

B2

11 1/2" Square

• Cut out the 22 1/2" squares of background fabric first.
• Cut these 22 1/2" squares twice diagonally as shown.
• Label the triangles B1.
• Cut out the 11 1/2" squares next.
• Cut these 11 1/2" squares once diagonally as shown.
• Label the triangles B2.

• Fold the 9 1/2" background squares in half diagonally.
• Place the Corner-14.5, page 45, Template on the fold of the 9 1/2" background squares.
• Cut the corner pieces as listed below.

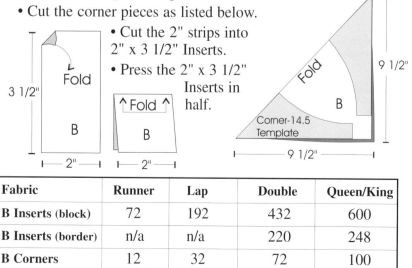

• Cut the 2" strips into 2" x 3 1/2" Inserts.
• Press the 2" x 3 1/2" Inserts in half.

Fabric	Runner	Lap	Double	Queen/King
B Inserts (block)	72	192	432	600
B Inserts (border)	n/a	n/a	220	248
B Corners	12	32	72	100

Cutting Wedges

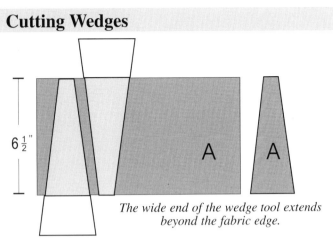

The wide end of the wedge tool extends beyond the fabric edge.

• Apply loops of wide transparent packaging tape, sticky side out, to the back of the Wedge Tool.

• Mark the 6 1/2" line, shown on page 44, on the Wedge Tool using a fine tipped permanent marker.

• Place the Wedge Tool on a 6 1/2" wide strip of Fabric A. Align the 6 1/2" mark with the fabric edge.

• From *each* of the *24* prints, cut the number of wedges listed below.

Runner	Lap	Double	Queen/King
3 wedges from each of 24 fabrics	8 wedges from each of 24 fabrics	19 wedges from each of 24 fabrics	26 wedges from each of 24 fabrics

Sewing Wedges

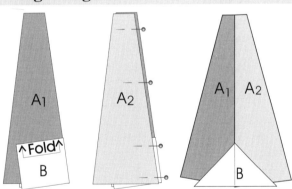

• Place a folded 2" x 3 1/2" B Insert onto a fabric wedge.

• Pin another fabric wedge on top.

• Sew the layers together.

• Repeat sewing wedge pairs together for *twelve* wedge pairs per block.

> *Double & King Note: Set aside the extra wedges for use later in the border*

Pressing Wedge Pairs

• From the back, lay the folded Inserts to one side and press the seam allowances open.

• Open up the B Insert, centering the fold line over the seam line and press.

Sewing Foursies

• Place a folded B Insert on a wedge pair.

• Pin another wedge pair on top.

• Sew the wedge pairs together to form a unit of four wedges, a "foursie".

• Repeat the steps to make *six* foursies per block.

Sewing Half Circles

• Place a folded B Insert onto a foursie unit.

• Pin another foursie unit on top.

• Sew the units together.

180 degrees

• Add another foursie unit to make a half circle.

• Press the half circle.

• Check to see that the half circle is straight.

If adjustment is necessary, see page 6 for suggestions.

• Repeat for the second half circle.

Sewing the Circle

• Place folded B Inserts along both edges of the half circle.

• Pin the other half on top.

• Sew the halves together.

• Press.

Center Applique

• Prepare the 2" circle applique found on page 47.

• Applique the circle over the center opening.

Adding Corners

• Sew *four* corner pieces together to make each corner unit.

• Pin the corner unit to the circle, matching seams.

• Sew the corner unit to the circle, with the circle against the bed of the sewing machine.

• Press the seam allowances toward the outside of the block.

Corners

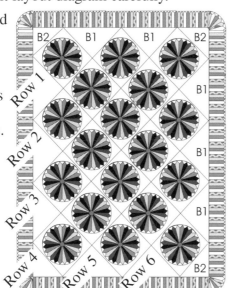

Corner Unit

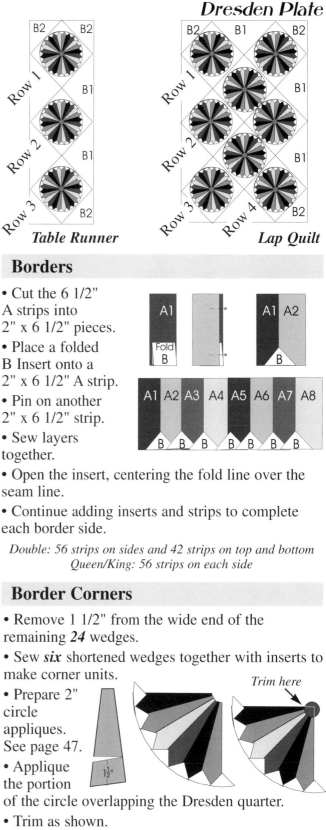

B2 B2

Row 1

B1

Row 2

B1

Row 3 B2

Table Runner

B2 B1 B2

Row 1

B1

Row 2

B1

Row 3 Row 4 B2

Lap Quilt

Assembling the Quilt

• Follow the quilt layout diagram carefully.

• Sew the B1 and B2 triangles to the appropriate squares.

• Sew the blocks and triangles together in rows.

• Sew the rows of blocks together.

B2 B1 B1 B2

Row 1

Row 2 B1

Row 3 B1

Row 4 Row 5 Row 6 B1

B2

Double Quilt

B2 B1 B1 B1 B2

Row 1

Row 2 B1

Row 3 B1

Row 4 Row 5 Row 6 Row 7 B1

B2

Queen/King Quilt

Borders

• Cut the 6 1/2" A strips into 2" x 6 1/2" pieces.

• Place a folded B Insert onto a 2" x 6 1/2" A strip.

• Pin on another 2" x 6 1/2" strip.

• Sew layers together.

A1
Fold
B

A1 A2
B

A1 A2 A3 A4 A5 A6 A7 A8
B B B B B B B

• Open the insert, centering the fold line over the seam line.

• Continue adding inserts and strips to complete each border side.

Double: 56 strips on sides and 42 strips on top and bottom
Queen/King: 56 strips on each side

Border Corners

• Remove 1 1/2" from the wide end of the remaining **24** wedges.

• Sew *six* shortened wedges together with inserts to make corner units.

• Prepare 2" circle appliques. See page 47.

Trim here

1 1/2"

• Applique the portion of the circle overlapping the Dresden quarter.

• Trim as shown.

Sewing Borders to Quilt

• Sew the side border strips to the corner pieces.

• Pin border strips to the quilt, adjusting if needed.

• Sew borders to the quilt.

Finishing

Refer to *Finishing* on page 6.

Amish Spiral

Fabric	Yardage	Strips to Cut
A	1/4 yd	THREE . . .1 3/4" wide strips
B	1/4 yd	THREE . . .1 3/4" wide strips
C	1/4 yd	THREE . . .1 3/4" wide strips
D	1/4 yd	THREE . . .1 3/4" wide strips
E	1/4 yd	THREE . . .1 3/4" wide strips
F	1/4 yd	THREE . . .1 3/4" wide strips
G	7/8 yd	THREE . . .1 3/4" wide strips
		ONE . . . . .4" wide strip
		ONE . . . . .12" square
Binding	3/8 yd	FOUR . . . . .2 1/2" bias strips
Fusible Web		1/4 yd . . . .
Batting		5/8 yd . . . .
Backing		5/8 yd . . . .
Binding		3/8 yd . . . .

Pictured on page 25 *Finished Size: 18" x 30"*

Preparing Templates and Wedge Tool

• Trace Templates A-S, A-M, A-L, and Corner-19 onto template plastic. See page 45 & 46.
• Apply loops of wide transparent tape, sticky side out, to the back of templates and Wedge Tool.

Cutting Strips

Note: The strips are cut across the fabric width (44-45").

• Cut the fabric strips as listed.
• Cut the 1 3/4" wide strips in half, making each 22" long.
• Label each strip. (i.e. A, B, C, D, E, F and G)

Cutting Corner Pieces

• Fold the 12" square of Fabric G diagonally.
• Place the Corner-19 Template on Fabric G.
• Cut *two* corner pieces.

Fold / G / Corner-19 / 12" / 12"

Preparing the Applique

• Trace the Amish applique found on page 48 onto the paper side of the fusible web.
• Iron the piece of fusible web to a piece of G fabric following manufacturer's instructions.
• Cut out the applique carefully following the traced lines.
• Set the applique aside for later placement.

Preparing the Inserts

• Cut *four* of each of the Amish Inserts.
• Fold each Amish Insert in half.
• Press the folds lightly.

Amish Inserts
*Cut **four** of each.*

Fold / Fold / Fold

A-S A-M A-L

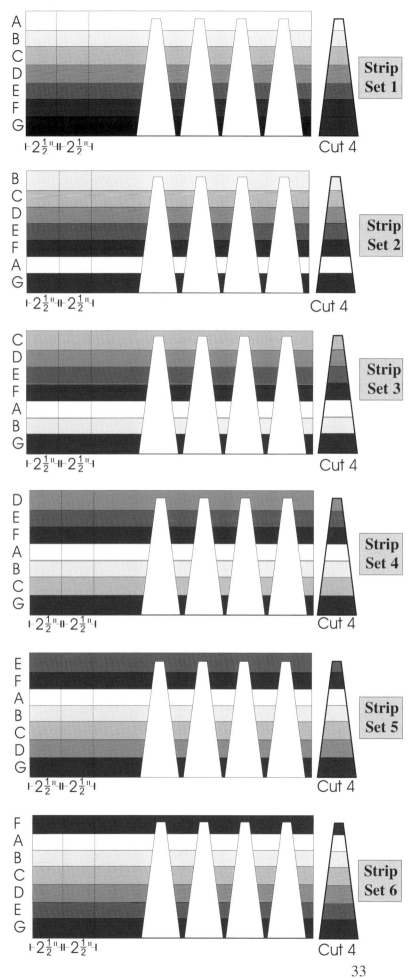

Strip Set 1 — A B C D E F G — 2½" — 2½" — Cut 4

Strip Set 2 — B C D E F A G — 2½" — 2½" — Cut 4

Strip Set 3 — C D E F A B G — 2½" — 2½" — Cut 4

Strip Set 4 — D E F A B C G — 2½" — 2½" — Cut 4

Strip Set 5 — E F A B C D G — 2½" — 2½" — Cut 4

Strip Set 6 — F A B C D E G — 2½" — 2½" — Cut 4

Sewing Strip Sets

• Sew *six* strip sets together in the order shown in the strip set diagrams.

Pressing Strip Sets

• From the back, press the seam allowances of Strip Sets #1, #3, and #5 *toward* the G strip.

• From the back, press the seam allowances of Strip Set #2, #4, and #6 *away* from the G strip.

• Label each strip set. *(i.e. 1, 2, 3, 4, 5 and 6)*

Cutting Wedges

• First, cut *two* 2 1/2" wide strips from each strip set and set aside.

• Place the Wedge Tool onto the strip set, aligning the wide end with the G strip.

• Cut *four* fabric wedges from each of the strip sets and label again.

— 2½"

Sewing Wedge Pairs

• Place the A-L Insert on Wedge #6.

• Pin Wedge #1 on top, right sides together.

• Sew the wedge pair together.

• Repeat sewing together #6 and #1 for a total of *four* pairs.

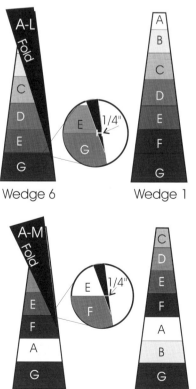

Wedge 6 (A-L Fold, C D E E G, 1/4") Wedge 1 (A B C D E F G)

Wedge 2 (A-M Fold, E F A G, 1/4") Wedge 3 (C D E F A B G)

33

- Place the A-M Insert onto Wedge #2 as shown on the previous page.
- Pin Wedge #3 on top, right sides together.
- Sew the wedge pair together.
- Repeat sewing #2 and #3 together for *four* pairs.
- Place the A-S Insert onto Wedge #4.
- Pin Wedge #5 on top, right sides together.
- Sew the wedge pair together.
- Repeat sewing #4 and #5 together for *four* pairs.

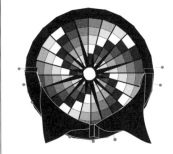

Wedge 4   Wedge 5

Sewing Quarter Circles

- Pin the **2-3** wedge pair onto the **6-1** wedge pair.
- Sew the pairs together to make a "foursie".
- Sew the **4-5** wedge pair to the **6-1/2-3** foursie, to form a quarter circle.
- Repeat for the remaining three quarters.

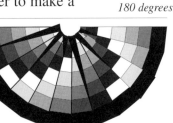

Sewing Halves

- Sew two quarters together to make a half circle.
- From the back, press the seam allowances of the half circle going in one direction.
- From the front, press the **inserts** going in one direction.

180 degrees

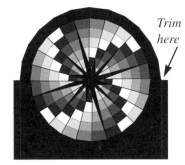

If adjustment is necessary, see page 6 for suggestions.

Sewing the Circle

- Sew the two halves together to make a circle.
- Press the circle.

Center Applique

- Prepare the 2" circle applique found on page 47.
- Applique the circle over the center opening.

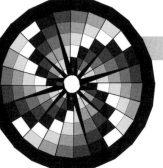

Sewing Corners

- Sew *two* corner pieces together.
- Pin the corner unit to the lower half of the circle, matching seams.
  - Sew the corner unit to the circle.
  - Trim the sides of the corner unit as shown.

Trim here

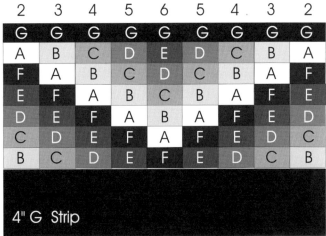

Assembling the Border Unit

- Lay out the 2 1/2" pieces following the order shown in the diagram below.
- Sew the border unit together.
- Sew the 4" Fabric G strip to the border unit.
- Iron the applique to the border unit.
- Sew the border unit to the circle unit.

|—2½"—|

2	3	4	5	6	5	4	3	2
G	G	G	G	G	G	G	G	G
A	B	C	D	E	D	C	B	A
F	A	B	C	D	C	B	A	F
E	F	A	B	C	B	A	F	E
D	E	F	A	B	A	F	E	D
C	D	E	F	A	F	E	D	C
B	C	D	E	F	E	D	C	B

4" G Strip

Finishing

Refer to *Finishing* on page 6.

Blue Corn Moon Variation

It's even simpler...

...the same basic design as the Amish Spiral, just omit the Inserts!

The border unit is slightly different, so follow the photograph on page 25 for the border arrangement.

Center Block

Fabric	Yardage	Strips to Cut
A	5/8 yd	TWO . . . 8 3/4" wide strips
B	1/2 yd	TWO . . . 6 1/2" wide strips
C	1/4 yd	ONE . . . . .5" wide strip
D	1/8 yd	ONE . . . . .3 1/2" wide strip
E	1/8 yd	ONE . . . . .2 1/4" wide strip
F	1/4 yd	ONE . . . . .5 1/2" square
G	1/3 yd	TWO . . . . .12" Squares

Borders

Fabric	Yardage	Strips to Cut
Border 1	1/8 yd	TWO . .1 1/4" wide strips
Border 2a	1/4 yd	ONE . . . .1 1/4" wide strip
2b		ONE . . . .5 1/2" wide strip
Lettering	1/8 yd	
Border 3	1/4 yd	FOUR . . . . .1" wide strips
Border 4	1/8 yd	ONE . . . .1 1/2" wide strip
Border 5*	1/4 yd	ONE . . . .7 1/2" wide strip
Border 6a	1/3 yd	TWO . .1 1/2" wide strips
6b		TWO . .2 1/2" wide strips
Binding	3/8 yd	FOUR . .2 1/2" wide strips
Fusible Web	1/8 yd	*If using a lengthwise
Batting	3/4 yd	stripe you'll need 3/4 yd*
Backing	1 yd	

Preparing Templates and Wedge Tool

• Trace templates B, C, D, and the Corner-19 onto template plastic, transferring lines. See page 45.
• Apply loops of wide transparent tape, sticky side out, to the back of the templates and the Wedge Tool.

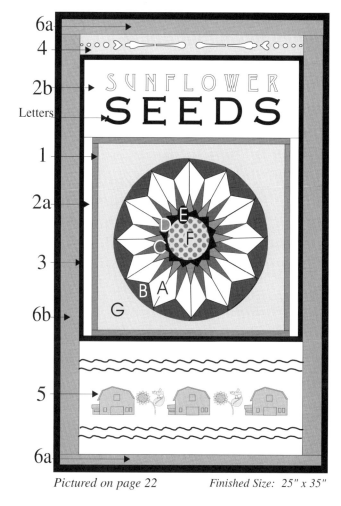

Pictured on page 22   *Finished Size: 25" x 35"*

Cutting Strips

• Cut the fabric strips as listed.

Note: The strips are cut across the fabric width (44-45").

Cutting Wedges

• Cut **24** fabric wedges from the 8 3/4" wide strips of Fabric A.

Cutting Corner Pieces

• Fold the 12" Fabric G squares diagonally.
• Place the Corner-19 Template along the fold of Fabric G.
• Cut **four** corner pieces.

Cutting Inserts

B Inserts

• Fold the 6 1/2" wide Fabric B strip in half lengthwise.

• Press fold.

• Place Template B along the fold.

• Cut *twelve* folded B Inserts.

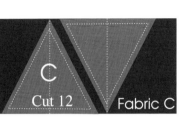

C Inserts

• Place Template C on the 5" wide strip of Fabric C.

• Cut *twelve* C Inserts.

D Inserts

• Place Template D on the 3 1/2" wide strip of Fabric D.

• Cut *twelve* D Inserts.

E Pieces

• Cut *twelve* 2 1/4" squares from the 2 1/4" wide strip of Fabric E.

E   Fabric E

$2\frac{1}{4}$"   *Cut twelve squares*

Pressing Inserts

C Inserts

• Fold the C Inserts in half, wrong sides together

• Press lightly along the fold.

D Inserts

• Fold the D Inserts in half, wrong sides together.

• Press lightly along the fold.

E Pieces

• Fold E squares in half diagonally, wrong sides together.

• Fold E in half again.

• Press the folds.

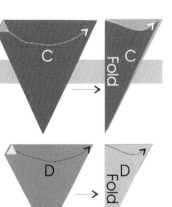

Note: Diagram's E pieces are enlarged

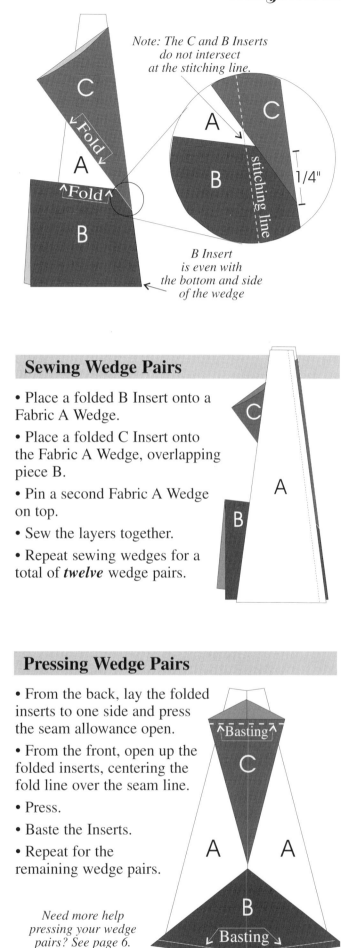

Note: The C and B Inserts do not intersect at the stitching line.

B Insert is even with the bottom and side of the wedge

Sewing Wedge Pairs

• Place a folded B Insert onto a Fabric A Wedge.

• Place a folded C Insert onto the Fabric A Wedge, overlapping piece B.

• Pin a second Fabric A Wedge on top.

• Sew the layers together.

• Repeat sewing wedges for a total of *twelve* wedge pairs.

Pressing Wedge Pairs

• From the back, lay the folded inserts to one side and press the seam allowance open.

• From the front, open up the folded inserts, centering the fold line over the seam line.

• Press.

• Baste the Inserts.

• Repeat for the remaining wedge pairs.

Need more help pressing your wedge pairs? *See page 6.*

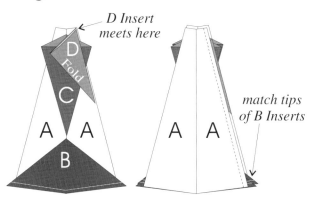

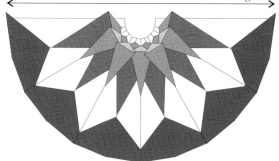

Sewing Foursies

• Place a folded D Insert onto a wedge pair, aligning it with the C Insert.

• Pin another wedge pair on top, matching the tips of the B Inserts.

• Sew the pairs together to form a unit of four wedges, "foursies".

Note: The tips of the C Insert are also sewn into this seam.

• Repeat to make *six* foursies.

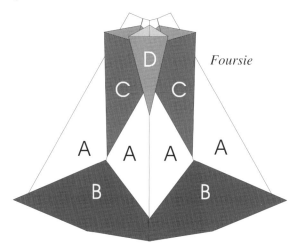

Foursie

Pressing Foursies

• From the back, lay the folded inserts to one side and press the seam allowance open.

• From the front, open up the folded inserts, centering the fold over the seam line. Press.

Sewing Half Circles

• Place a folded D Insert onto a foursie unit.

• Pin another foursie unit on top.

• Sew the foursies together.

• Place another D Insert onto the unit of eight.

• Sew a foursie to this piece to make a half circle.

• Repeat for the second half circle.

Pressing the Half Circles

• Press the half circle carefully.

• Using a large ruler, check to see that the half circle is straight.

• Repeat for the other half circle.

If adjustment is necessary, see page 6 for suggestions.

180 degrees

Sewing the Circle

• Place folded D Inserts onto the half circle.

• Pin the other half circle on top.

• Sew the halves together.

• Press the seams open from the back.

• Press the D inserts open from the front.

Preparing the Center Applique

• Prepare the 4 1/2" circle applique found on page 47 using the 5 1/2" square of Fabric F.

Adding E Pieces

• Pin the folded Fabric E pieces around the center opening, inserting one E piece into the next one.

• Use the Seed Packet center applique as a guide to check the position of the E pieces.

• Baste the E pieces in place.

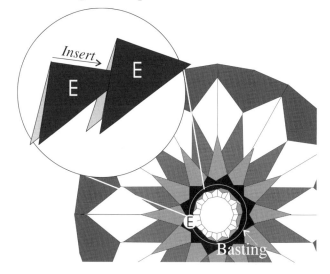

Adding the Center Applique

• Center the 4 1/2"
circle applique over
the center opening in
the circular block.

• Hand or machine
applique the circle
applique onto the
block.

Adding Corners

• Sew the four corner
pieces together.

• Pin the corner unit
onto the pieced circle,
matching seams.

• Sew the corner unit
to the circle with the
circle against the bed
of the sewing machine and the corner unit on top.

• Press the seam allowances toward the outside of
the square.

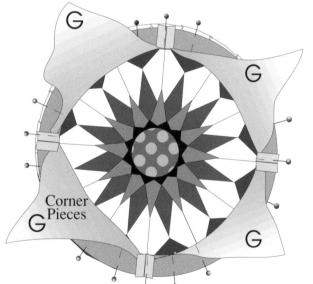

Making B Inserts Curved

• To create a curved
edge, roll back the fold
of the B inserts.

• Press the curved fold
in place.

• Top stitch the fold
in place, using an
applique or decorative
stitch.

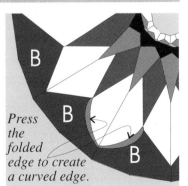

*Press
the
folded
edge to create
a curved edge.*

Lettering

• Trace the lettering found on page 47 onto the
paper side of the fusible web.

• Iron fusible web onto the back of the lettering
fabric.

• Cut the letters out precisely following the lines

• Arrange the lettering onto Border 2b.

• Fuse the lettering onto Border 2b following the
fusible web manufacturer's instructions.

Adding Borders

• Sew a Border 1 strip along
one side of the flower square,
right sides together.

• Press the seams toward the
outside.

• Trim the Border 1 strip
even with the square.

• Repeat adding Border 1
strips for the opposite side,
top and bottom.

• Sew the Border 2a strips to
the left and right sides. Trim.

Border 1

• Sew the Border 2b strip to the top. Trim.

• Sew the Border 3 to the sides, top and bottom.
Trim.

• Sew the Border 4 strip to the top. Trim.

• Sew the Border 5 strip to the bottom. Trim.

• Sew Border 6b strips to the left and right sides.
Trim.

• Sew
Border 6a
strips to the
top and
bottom.
Trim.

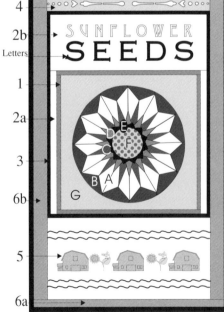

Finishing

Refer to *Finishing* on page 6.

The Birdhouse

A Variation of the Seed Packet

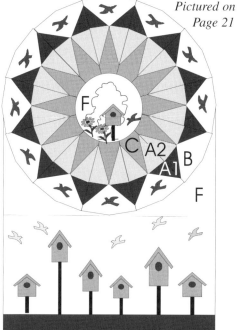

Pictured on Page 21

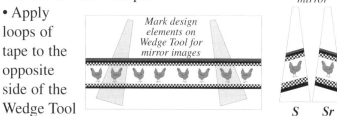

Finished size: 19" x 28"

Fabric	Yardage	Strips to Cut
A1	1/4 yd	TWO . . .3 1/2" wide strips
A2	1/4 yd	ONE . . . . . .6" wide strips
B*	1/2 yd	TWO . . . . . .6 1/2" strips
C	1/4 yd	ONE . . . . . . .5" wide strip
Note: Fabrics D and E are omitted		
F	3/8 yd	ONE . . . . . . .5 1/2" square
		ONE . . . . .12" square
Border	1/3 yd	ONE . . . . .9" x 19" strip
Binding	3/8 yd	2 1/2" bias strips
Batting	2/3 yd	*The bird motif is centered*
Backing	2/3 yd	*on B pieces*

• Sew the A1-A2 Strip Set as shown.
• Cut **24** wedges aligning the 6" line, page 44, with the A1-A2 seam.
• Cut *twelve* B Inserts and *twelve* C Inserts, page 45.
• Cut *two* Corner-19 pieces, page 45, from Fabric F.
• Refer to the *Seed Packet* instructions for block assembly.
• Sew *two* corner pieces together.
• Sew the corner unit to the circle.
• Add the 9" wide Border strip.
• Refer to *Finishing* on page 6.

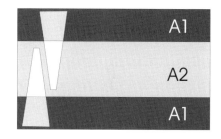

Fabric	Yardage	Strips to Cut
A	2/3 yd*	*May need more fabric to match stripes*
B	1/2 yd	TWO . . . 6 1/2" wide strips
C	1/4 yd	ONE . . . . .5" wide strip
Note: Fabric D is omitted		
E	1/8 yd	ONE . . . . .2 1/4" wide strip
F	1/4 yd	ONE . . . . .8" square
G	3/8 yd	ONE . . . . .12" squares
		ONE . . . . .4" x 9" strip
Border	1/3 yd	ONE . . . . .6 1/2" x 19"
Binding	3/8 yd	
Batting	2/3 yd	
Backing	2/3 yd	

Sunny Side Up

A Variation of the Seed Packet

• Cut *two* Corner-19 pieces, page 45, from Fabric G.
• Refer to the *Seed Packet* instructions, pages 35-38, for block assembly.
• Applique a 6 1/2" circle of Fabric F over the center opening. See page 44.
• Sew *two* corner pieces together.
• Sew the corner unit to the circle.
• Add the 6 1/2" wide Border strip and the 4" Fabric G strip.
• Refer to *Finishing* on page 6.

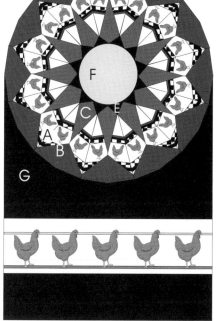

Pictured on page 21
Finished Size: 19" x 30"

• Trace the S line, page 44, onto the Wedge Tool.
• Cut *twelve* S wedges from Fabric A, aligning the S line to the border stripe.
• Apply loops of tape to the opposite side of the Wedge Tool and turn it over.
• Cut *twelve* Sr mirror image wedges from Fabric A.
• Cut *twelve* B and *twelve* C Inserts and *twelve* E Pieces, page 45.

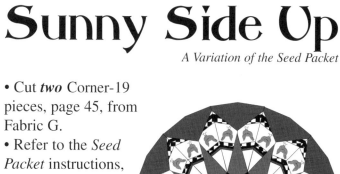

Mark design elements on Wedge Tool for mirror images

mirror

S *Sr*

Persian Star

Quilt Size: 70" x 100"   *8 blocks*

Fabric	Yardage	Strips to Cut
A	3 1/4 yd	TWENTY FOUR .4 1/2" strips
B	2 1/4 yd	SIXTEEN .....4 1/2" strips
P	2 yd	EIGHT ....9" strips
S	1/2 yd	THREE ......4 1/4" strips
E	3/4 yd*	*minimum amount-**six** design repeats
F	4 3/8 yd	SIXTEEN .....12" squares
		TWO ....32" squares
		TWO ....17" squares
Piping	1/2 yd	ONE ....14 1/2" strip
Lattice	3/4 yd	TWELVE ....2" strips
Border 1	1/3 yd	EIGHT ......1" wide strips
Border 2	3/4 yd	NINE ....2 1/2" strips
Border 3	1 1/4 yd	TEN ....4" wide strips
Batting	3 yd	(90" wide)
Backing	6 yd	
Binding	3/4 yd	

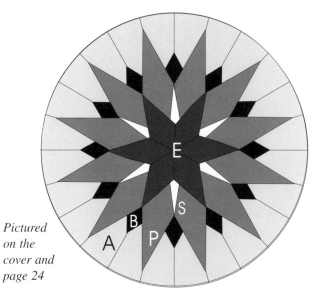

Pictured on the cover and page 24

Cutting Strips

• Cut the fabric strips and squares as listed.
Note: Strips are cut across the fabric width (44-45").

Cutting Corner Pieces

• Fold the Fabric F squares diagonally.
• Place the Corner-19 Template on the fold line.
• Cut **32** corner pieces.

Preparing Templates and Wedge Tool

• Trace Templates P, S, the Star Point and the Corner-19 onto template plastic. See pages 45 & 46.
• Trace the Q Line onto the Wedge Tool. See page 44.
• Apply loops of wide transparent tape, sticky side out, to the back of the templates and the Wedge Tool.

Cutting Background Pieces

• Cut the 17" F squares **once** diagonally.
• Cut the 32" F squares **twice** diagonally.
• Label the triangles F1 and F2 as shown.
Note: Two triangles are left over.

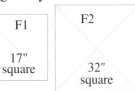

Cutting Inserts

P Inserts

• Place Template P on the 9" wide P strip.
• Cut **twelve** P Inserts per block. *(96 total)*
• Fold the P Inserts in half, wrong sides together.
• Press the folds lightly.

S Inserts

• Place Template S on the 4 1/4" wide S strip.
• Cut **six** S Inserts for each block. *(48 total)*
• Fold the S Inserts in half, wrong sides together.
• Press lightly along the fold.

Star Points

• For a kaleidoscope effect, use a set of mirrors to select the design placement of the Star Point on Fabric E. A paper window *(see page 46)* is also helpful in design selection.
• Draw a part of the fabric design onto the template with a fine tipped marker. Use these lines to reposition the star template in the same place to get **exact** duplicates.
• Cut **six** identical Star Points for each block.

Sewing the Center Star

• Fold the Star Points in half, right sides together.

• Press lightly along the folds.

• Sew along the outer tip sides of the Star Points, leaving a 6" tail of thread.

• Cut away the folded tip as shown in the diagram.

• Thread a needle with the thread tail.

• Insert the needle into the center point between the fabric layers.

• Using the thread tail, pull the star point inside out, gently tugging on the thread to make the tip sharp.

• Leave the thread tail attached for use later.

• Repeat for the remaining points.

• Pin two Star Points together.

• Sew the points together.

• Press the seams open with each added seam.

• Add a third point to make a star half.

• Repeat for a second star half.

• Sew halves together, matching the center.

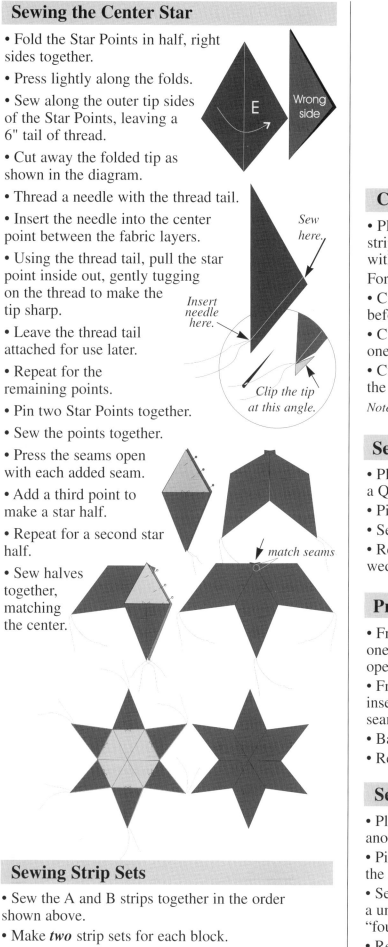

Sewing Strip Sets

• Sew the A and B strips together in the order shown above.

• Make *two* strip sets for each block.

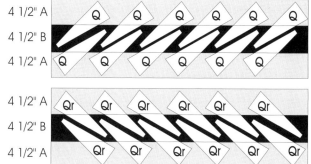

Cutting Wedges

• Place the wedge tool onto the strips set, matching Line Q with the AB seam.

For each block:

• Cut wedges up and down before moving laterally.

• Cut *twelve* Q wedges from one ABA strip set.

• Cut *twelve* Qr wedges from the other ABA strip set.

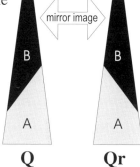

Note: The Qr wedges are the mirror image of the Q wedges.

Sewing Wedge Pairs

• Place a folded P Insert onto a Q fabric wedge.

• Pin a Qr fabric wedge on top.

• Sew the layers together.

• Repeat for a total of *twelve* wedge pairs per block.

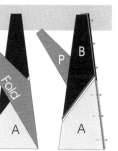

Pressing Wedge Pairs

• From the back, lay the folded inserts to one side, and press the seam allowance open.

• From the front, open up the folded inserts, centering the fold over the seam line. Press.

• Baste the P Insert across the top.

• Repeat for remaining wedge pairs.

Sewing Foursies

• Place one wedge pair on top of another wedge pair.

• Pin the pairs together, matching the AB seam and the P Inserts.

• Sew pairs together to form a unit of four wedges, "foursies".

• Repeat for *six* foursies.

a foursie

Adding S Inserts

• Place a folded S Insert onto a foursie.

• Pin another foursie on top, matching the AB seams and the P Inserts.

• Sew the foursies together, for a unit of eight wedges.

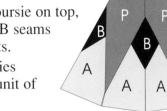

Sewing Half Circles

• Pin a folded S Insert onto this unit of eight wedges.

• Pin another foursie unit on top, matching the AB seams and P Inserts.

180 degrees

• Sew on another foursie to make a half circle.

• Repeat for the second half circle.

Pressing Half Circles

• Press the half circle carefully.

• Using a large ruler, check to see it is straight.

• Repeat for the other half circle.

If adjustment is necessary, see page 6 for suggestions.

Sewing Circles

• Place folded S Inserts onto the half circle.

• Pin the other half circle on top.

• Sew the halves together.

• Press the seam allowances open from the back.

• From the front, open the S Inserts and press.

Appliqueing the Star Center

• Pin the star applique over the center opening, aligning the star points with the wedge seams as shown.

• Using the thread tails attach each Star Point to the circle at the wedge seam line.

• Applique by machine or hand.

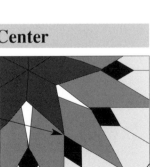

Cutting Piping

• For each block, cut *three* 1" wide bias strips from the 14 1/2" wide piping fabric strip.

• Sew *three* 1" wide bias strips together for each block.

• Measure and cut 60" of bias per block.

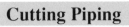

Sew here to join bias strips.

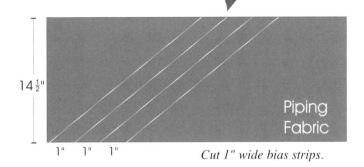

$14\frac{1}{2}$"

Piping Fabric

1" 1" 1"

Cut 1" wide bias strips.

Adding Piping

• Join the ends to form a 60" bias loop.

• Fold the bias loop in half lengthwise, wrong sides together.

• Press.

• Fold the loop into quarters and mark with pins.

• Pin the bias loop to the circle, raw edges together, matching the quarter marks with the 6th, 12th, 18th and 24th seam.

• Sew the bias piping to the circle.

piping

Adding Corners

• Sew four corner pieces together.

• Pin the corner unit onto the pieced circle matching seams.

• Sew the corner unit to the circle with the circle against the bed of the sewing machine and the corner unit on top.

• Press the seam allowances toward the outside of the square.

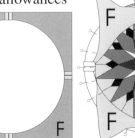

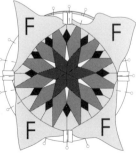

Sewing Blocks and Lattice

- Sew lattice strips to the sides of the blocks referring to the quilt diagram.
- Sew the blocks and triangles together in rows.
- Sew the remaining lattice strips between the block rows.
- Trim the corner triangles 6 1/2" from the lattice edge.

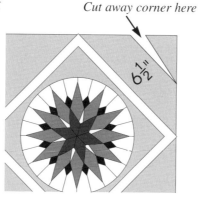

Cut away corner here

$6\frac{1}{2}"$

Adding Borders

- Sew Border #1 to the corners.
- Trim the Border in line with the quilt sides as shown.

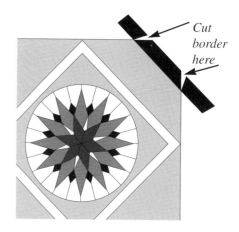

Cut border here

- Sew the border strips to the sides of the quilt.
- Cut away these border strips in line with the corner borders as shown.
- Repeat for Border #2.

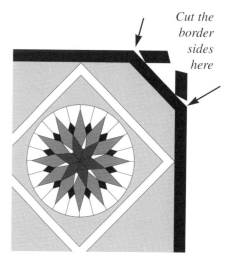

Cut the border sides here

Finishing

Refer to the *Finishing* instructions found on page 6.

F1   F2   F1

Row 1

F2

Row 2

F2

F2

Row 3   Row 4   F1

Santa Banner

A One Block Variation of the Persian Star

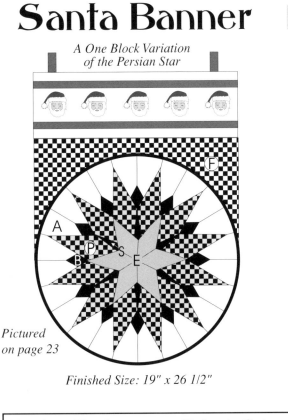

Pictured on page 23

Finished Size: 19" x 26 1/2"

Making the Tabs

• Fold the 3" x 7" Fabric B strips in half, right sides together.
• Sew along the edge as shown.
• Turn the tube right side out.

Sew here

fold —————7"—————

• Center the seam.
• Tuck the raw edges into the tube.
• Press.
• Form a loop.
• Repeat for the second tab.
• Hand sew the tabs to the back of the banner for hanging.

Wedge Tool

Q Line

6" Line

6 1/2" Line

S Line

Fabric	Yardage	Strips to Cut
A	5/8 yd	FOUR . . . . . . .4 1/2" strips
B	3/8 yd	TWO . . . . . . .4 1/2" strips
		TWO . . . . . . .3" x 7" strips
P	1/3 yd	ONE . . . . .9" strip
S	1/4 yd	ONE . . . . . . .4 1/4" strip
E	1/4 yd*	*minimum amount-- **six** design repeats*
F	3/8 yd	ONE . . . . .12" square
Piping	1/2 yd	ONE . . . . . . .7 1/2" strip
Piping	1/4 yd	ONE . . . .8 1/2" x 19" strip
Border	5/8 yd	
Batting	2/3 yd	
Backing	2/3 yd	
Binding	1/2 yd	

• Follow the *Persian Star* instructions to make the circular block.
• Cut *six* 1" bias strips from the 7 1/2" wide piping fabric.

See page 42 for piping instructions.

• Sew *two* corner pieces together to form a half corner.
• Sew the half corner unit to the circle.
• Sew the border piece to the corner unit.
• For *Finishing* refer to page 6.

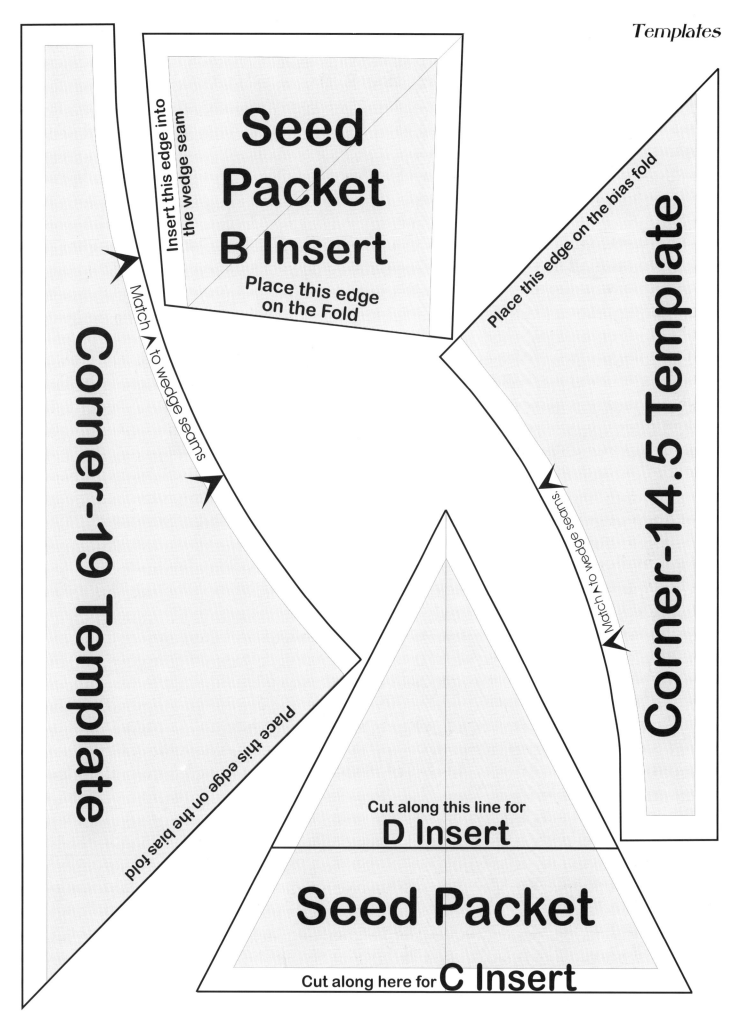

Corner-19 Template

Seed Packet B Insert

Insert this edge into the wedge seam

Place this edge on the Fold

Match to wedge seams

Place this edge on the bias fold

Corner-14.5 Template

Place this edge on the bias fold

Match to wedge seams.

Cut along this line for D Insert

Seed Packet

Cut along here for C Insert

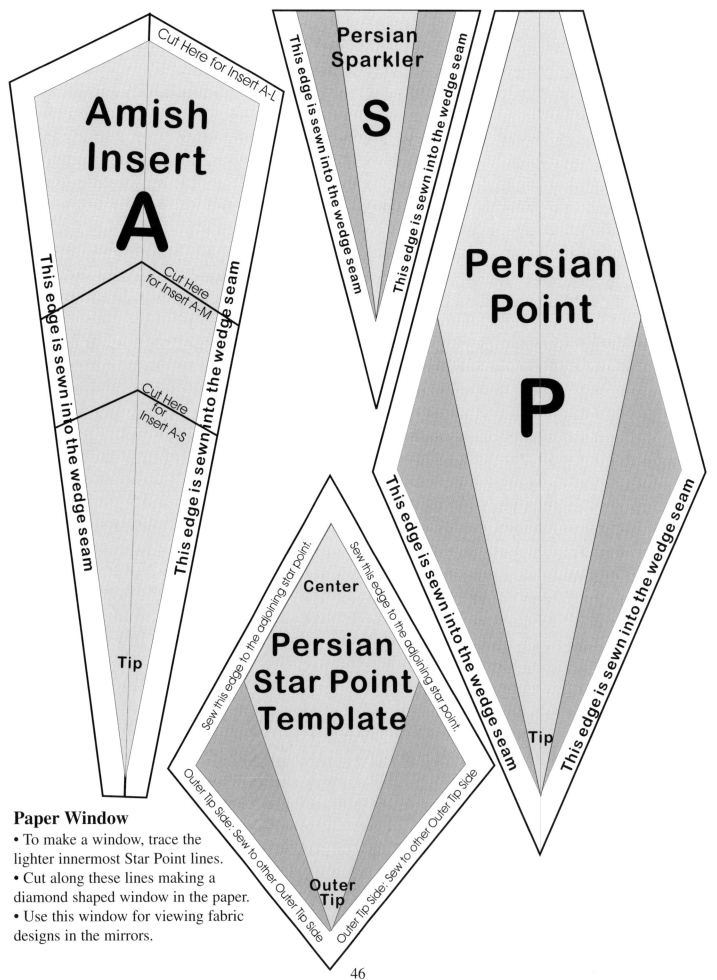

Amish Insert A

Cut Here for Insert A-L

This edge is sewn into the wedge seam

Cut Here for Insert A-M

This edge is sewn into the wedge seam

Cut Here for Insert A-S

Tip

Persian Sparkler S

This edge is sewn into the wedge seam

This edge is sewn into the wedge seam

Persian Point P

This edge is sewn into the wedge seam

This edge is sewn into the wedge seam

Tip

Persian Star Point Template

Center

Sew this edge to the adjoining star point.

Sew this edge to the adjoining star point.

Outer Tip Side: Sew to other Outer Tip Side

Outer Tip Side: Sew to other Outer Tip Side

Outer Tip

Paper Window
- To make a window, trace the lighter innermost Star Point lines.
- Cut along these lines making a diamond shaped window in the paper.
- Use this window for viewing fabric designs in the mirrors.

Circle Appliques

Cut here
for watermelon

2"

3 1/2"

4 1/2"

6 1/2"

*Letters are
mirrored and
thus ready to be
traced onto
fusible web.*

Trace 2 E letters

Trace 2 S letters

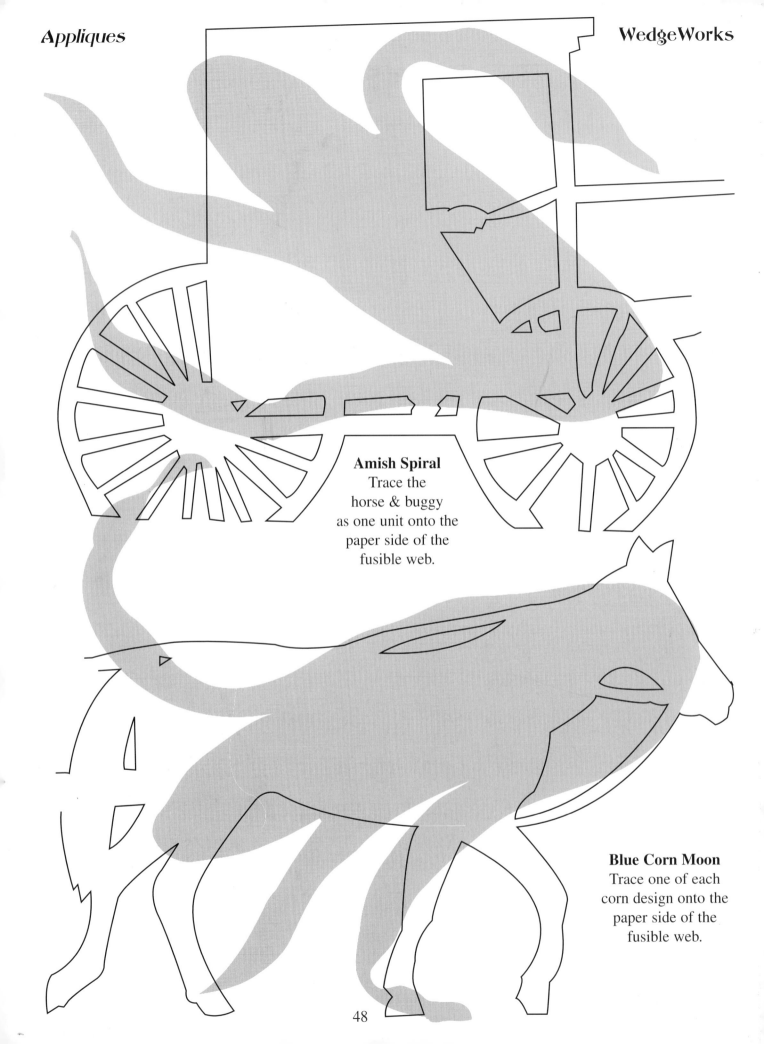

Amish Spiral
Trace the
horse & buggy
as one unit onto the
paper side of the
fusible web.

Blue Corn Moon
Trace one of each
corn design onto the
paper side of the
fusible web.